Picture

of

Me

Thomas Laurence

Picture of Me
Copyright © 2024 by Thomas Laurence

ISBN: 978-1962497480(sc)
ISBN: 978-1962497497(e)

The Reading Glass Books
BOOKS

The Reading Glass Books
1-888-420-3050
www.readingglassbooks.com
fulfillment@readingglassbooks.com

Contents

Prologue

"Your mother has been killed in a car accident"

I sat there, gazing back into my fathers' eyes as his words shocked me to my very core. Little did I know, when I left for school that morning, that was the last time I would see my mother alive. My sister Julie and I were both in middle school together, so we were both summoned to the principal's office at the same time.

"Will Julie and Thomas Laurence please report to the principal's office"

I was not a trouble maker at the time, so I can honestly say that I was extremely curious as to why I was being called upon, but never suspected it would change my life forever.

That morning was not much different than any other morning. My three sisters and I were up late as usual, so the hustle began immediately. My mother was trying to assist all of us in getting ready for our school day, while also trying to get herself prepped for her day. She was attending a graduate program to get her nursing degree, an aspiration she had for quite a while. She was three months away from graduating said program. It was always stressful for my mother when we lackadaisically moped around each morning to catch the bus to school. At this point in our lives, she was likely getting used to it, but it's still never easy to deal with on your own, especially with four of us. There is strength in numbers! My mother had been on her own for two years now since my parents divorced. In contrast to before the split, she did not have to get ready for a job of her own, as we were her job. Tensions always ran high in our household on a school morning.

It did not happen very often, but on this morning, my sister Julie and I missed our bus. My mother was also running late due to our inability to hustle and need for constant reminders.

"Did you eat"?

"Did you brush your teeth"?

"Do you have your homework in your bag"?

The usual nagging from a caring, yet distracted with her own problems, kind of mother. She did not have time to drive us. Our school was approximately a mile from our house, and it was March 15th after all, we were in the throes of a dead freeze. Typical Massachusetts winter. The very thought of walking that mile to then sit in classrooms for eight hours was a bitter one. For two middle schoolers, me being 13 and Julie being 15, that bitterness came out with anger and nasty comments toward my mother. But again, this was a semi-typical morning in the Laurence post-divorce household. Things were said. Things that would resonate in us for years, and like we used to say as children, there are no take backsies.

So, off we went. The freeze had taken complete control of the ground. The sidewalks were mother nature's skating rink, with mounds of dirty snow on both sides. I do not remember the exact degree, but it felt like negative 15 degrees to me.

Within minutes, the chill had my ears and nose stinging, and the shiver that takes complete control of your body, set in with a ferocity. We walked side by side, quickly at first, but the longer you are in the cold, the slower your footsteps seem to get, no matter how badly you just want to reach your destination. That is when the voice inside my head started to curse my mother. How could she not even care that we are freezing half to death? She is in her nice warm car on her way to school. She seriously could not go a little out of her way? She obviously does not care about us. I am never talking to her, ever again!

Well, my friends, that last thought in my head was what I remember the most. I never legitimately thought it would be a true statement, nor did I want it to be. I loved my mom. But petty things, like having to walk to school (when it was my own darn fault), get the best of us sometimes, and we do and say things as a result that can never be undone. Typically speaking, most people on most days can get away with it. But not us, not on this particular morning. It's the little things that haunt us the most sometimes. That final interaction with my mother would stick with me for a long time.

When my father told me what happened, it was like an explosion, an instant rush of pain followed by numbness and disbelief. My body went into shock. It is the fight or flight response, and my body and mind automatically chose flight. I needed to soar above the intense pain, and pretend it was not really happening. This was NOT reality!

The rest of the day was a blur. I remember bits and pieces of the events that took place throughout the day, but from the moment I was told, to when we arrived at my two oldest sisters' school, I remember nothing. I was shut down, in a completely different universe than where I started my day.

We walked into the main office of Assabet Valley High School, to where they took us to a small conference room with a window facing the school parking lot. Julie and I sat on the floor, while my father and my uncle stood near the window. My sister Cathy was the first one to arrive after getting a similar announcement as Julie and I did over the loud speaker. She had an apple in hand, and was taking a bite as she walked in. She was surprised to see my father, my uncle and the two of us in the room, and made a comment to us about it.

"Wow, what are you all doing here"?

She looked around the room at each of us individually, toggling back and forth, waiting for an answer. It was only for a moment, but it seemed like an eternity. Mercifully, my father finally broke the silence that was killing me, and came out with the reason we were all gathered. Cathy gasped inwardly, and the apple that she was chewing went down her throat and she choked for a second before being able to dislodge and swallow it. Then came the outburst, and I watched in horror as I witnessed the same terror in my sister that I felt myself, just an hour before. It was like reliving the moment again after I successfully numbed myself and fell into denial. It made it all too real.....again.

After a while, my oldest sister, Mary, came strolling in. She took one look at all of us in our emotionally shattered state, and she knew. I remember her falling to the floor, collapsing, like it was not even in her control, and screaming, "What happened to mom"? Nobody had to say a word. She too, was inconsolable, and once again the rest of us fed off that. It was like an assembly line of pain.

The making of a nightmare, really. You do not expect these things to happen to you. We all know death is imminent, and possible, even likely, in so many ways, but nothing prepares you for accidental death. There is no "dealing with death for dummies" book. And, even if there was, I was an immature 13 year old boy, so you would not be able to dumb it down enough for my brain.

We were at my sister's school for quite a while, although I really do not remember why we lingered so long. I needed a break, and to detach myself from my surroundings. I remember going into the bathroom, a single bathroom near the conference room we were in, and locking the door behind me. I was again, trying to work myself into a numb state, but I could not stop my thoughts anymore.

They would NOT STOP! I sat with my back against the wall underneath the paper towel dispenser and stared straight ahead. The gravity of this situation was really starting to sink in. I thought about my mother, and nothing else. At a certain point, my vision went fuzzy in an almost white vision, and I lost it. I screamed, and I kicked and punched anything around me, and burst out into violent tears and sobbing. My decimal had to be nightmarish for anyone who had been listening. I had lost control of myself. It all hit me in the face at that moment in time. I will never see mom again. She is gone, and I am helpless to change that.

I think part of my soul left me that day.

To be continued.......

Poetry

Picture of you

I can picture your baby blue caravan,

so innocent in its journey.

An angelic rider,

who complimented the world

with a radiant presence.

Arduous labor

and continuous search for love,

were a source

of your discontent.

Protector of mischievous children,

was your incentive

to go on.

I can picture

your gentle smile

that brought the sun

to my growing darkness.

You always had a way
of taking away the pain.

I can picture the fear
displayed on your beautiful face,
as you slid to the other side.

One fatal moment,
over in a flash,
like your life was expendable.

The cataclysm of my life.

Like a shipwrecked fool,
I was lost without my compass.

I was beaten and broken,
with bitter resentments.

Four notches up on my timeline,
I cannot picture you
anymore.

Like a forgotten dream,

which once held

great importance.

All I have now,

is a stone engraved

with your name.

I'm haunted

with morbid thoughts and feelings

and bothered

by an unforgiving record.

I can't stand you helpless,

no better than the dirt.

Surrounded by a lifeless shell,

worms abound

upon your rotting forehead.

The sky is beautiful right now

above your home,

and around your quarters.

Mournful cronies come,

and quickly leave.

I wish not to be here anymore.

I will see you

one more time before I go.

My departure

will be sad and lonely.

I'm going to try to be somebody.

Somebody,

a mother can love.

Dark Knight

I looked over

at my disfigured shadow

peering back at me,

dark and expressionless,

as if to tell me

of things to come.

It seems

this elusive creature

has been following me.

Shrinking

and

disappearing,

curiously,

as if to taunt me.

It speaks to me,

savagely.

Tells me how mystical

its world can be.

"Follow me to the end

and you'll be free".

The temptation overwhelmed

my capacity to think,

and the world slipped away.

The dark knight

is a step ahead of me,

and is there

to stay.

Waiting......Patiently

Always

Incomprehensible is he,

yet,

I sense that I've known him,

personally,

since the start of my days.

Friend or Foe?????

A fever,

construed as sickness.

You get hot,

you need a fix,

to be fixed.

They'll tell you you're normal,

to subside that feeling of guilt,

so you do it again,

and it becomes your friend.

You start to depend

on a euphoria,

to keep you going,

to lend a hand.

They give you the upper hand,

while the underside

is hidden,

so you can hide,

in comfort.

Mothers Disgrace

It doesn't take long to feel displaced,
when you're a fallen child.

Mothers' disgrace.

Good deeds have been erased
from countless actions,
made in poor taste.

Too far in the weeds
to get back in good grace,
the world seems better off
if I was erased.

Buzz on the streets;
conversations in the hollow;
it's a dangerous game
that's best not to follow.

But follow I do,

and trouble pursues

to the end of each day.

Then arises anew.

Nothing different

is ever on the morrow.

Only the pain

and predestined sorrow.

Random thoughts pt. 1

Surrender to your needs,

and all the power you want,

shall rise.

If you can live with nothing,

you can live with anything.

< >

The man keeps the carousel going

around in his head.

When the power source is empty,

so is his motivation.

The struggle is daily,

and his mind grows weaker.

<-Wrong way of a one way<-

The bum on the street,

means so much to me.

He is my friend,

you're the enemy.

The end of life

as I know it to be,

starts with you.

I need a change,

something new.

But it's all the same

point of view.

I'm sick of the past,

it's killing me.

I have no future,

it's meant to be.

Dreams Become Reality

I suffer from daydreaming,

a yearning,

to be something else.

I've dreamt up

some pretty marvelous images

for myself.

Better than a movie can show.

Little did I know, my imagination

would be powerful forthcomings

in my life.

What a painful day

to wake up and realize

the metamorphosis is complete.

My fantasies

have become

my fallacies.

My comfort resides in an uncertainty;

an excitement to keep me going

through the monotony

that is known

as life.

Lonely Song

Deep in space,
but out of time.
Having fun,
but bored out of my mind.

I used to be hated,
but now the hate is mine.
I used to love my neighbor,
but now he can die.

I used to wake up happy,
but now I'm too tired.
I used to love freedom,
but that's not around.

I used to love to talk,
but all the words are gone.

All there's left is nothing,
but to sing my lonely song.

Soul to Keep

I pray the lord my soul to keep,

and not get lost in the cloud

that envelops me.

Rising from the fire below,

a billowing demise,

blinding my eyes

with burning desire.

I have not chosen

to sell out my soul....

I believe.

But if I do,

it will come with a price,

and the tag is not cheap.

I want charisma,

fortune and fame.

I want to be handsome

and never age.

Life full of pride

and pleasurable sin.

Every battle I enter,

I come out with a win.

I want intelligence,

and power.

I will not be an average man,

the world will pay attention,

and cower.

The endless list of desire

can never be satisfied,

nor it be tamed,

once it's been fueled

by temptations flame.

When your fire dies out

and all is lost

it's your soul that it takes,

when you're body is tossed.

Random thoughts pt. 2

Sometimes,

it's hard to tell the truth.

Sometimes,

it's hard to tell a lie.

Seldom are we clear with answers,

answers pass us by.

< >

First time I see you

in the morning,

makes me sick.

Hungover,

I mix the thoughts in my mind.

Unrealistically think I can survive,

under this microscope,

where anything applies.

Life and Death

Life is an arduous thing,
and people know their limitations
yet, challenge them.
The bitter knowledge of near death,
                    gives meaning,
and excites shallow bodies.

Origami

Baptize my tongue

with your poison game.

Am I too young?

Will I ever be the same?

Through the pages of my mind,

through the pages of knowledge and time,

comes rushing

an intense wave of energy.

Like a white squall   or a tsunami.

Turns those pages

into origami.

Coming of Age

Too much confusion,

the patterns,

setting in.

Fitting in seems a long road.

In every which way,

I should be blooming.

Which seems pointless,

when every flower must die,

and ascend

to that garden in the sky.

Sometimes, I do cry for the sun

to keep me strong,

and healthy,

while I am peaking.

But freaking out

causes doubt.

This seems

to be a passion

meant for someone else.

Chambers

Outside my door,

I stand,

looking in.

At what could be me,

peeking out.

Waiting for a brighter day

to release me

From these chambers.

Six feet under her spell

Six heads in a field,

ten seconds....

a moment of silence.

Enter music, rhythmic movement.

Passion for a girl, unspent.

Green eyes, brown hair.

Face to die for.

Reputation for destruction.

She caught wind of my gaze,

unfolding the desire I hold,

and cracked a smile,

removing my self-control.

It was that moment I realized

that if I indulge,

it just may be

what ends up killing me.

The Captain & Me

How lonely it is at sea,
the captain and me.

Searching a world
of tiny people,
with our fishing net,
and a string with a hook.

Have I ever caught anything good?

I don't think I have.

This appears to be all there is
under the far and beyond skies,
as we sail through a giant
ocean of lies.

Random thoughts pt. 3

The bond that ties us together
is what's tearing us apart.

< >

Fuck that commotion
that's causing my ears to bleed.
The world can't compare.
From the inside,
the noise is louder.

< >

I see light eyes,
but dark souls.
Confusion.
Panic.
We are lost.
Ever
So
Lost.

A Pen~

Just give me a pen,

that's all I need.

I don't need people,

just a pen.

It's pointless to talk to them.

Nothing comes back.

I get no pleasure,

no relief.

Maybe a lie or two,

or three.

They never mean

what they say.

So,

who needs people?

I don't.

Tilt

Stuck in my head
for far too long.
Wasting away
my very own time.

Not too far
from completely gone.
This time on loan,
I've borrowed too long.

Trapped in the jail,
that no one else can see.
Constrained by my thoughts,
never destined to be free.

Confined by my fear
and paralyzing guilt.

The end is near,
my life is on tilt.

No help for the Wicked

Nothing but a product
of a father's fury,
and mother extenuates the pain.

There is no choice,
but to go insane.

Us children of despair,
have lost right
to our happiness,
through the eyes of our creator.

Help has not found us,
and it never will.

Falling on deaf ears,
our hearts have spilled.

Seek.....

and you shall find nothing;

Ask.....

and you shall receive punishment;

Knock.....

and the door will open to your fears;

Truth kills,

and lies reign forever.

This is hell,

and there is no heaven.

Relinquish our hopes,

and keep rehashing

our pathetic lives.

Earth is facing

its biggest downfall.

Where is our savior now??

Schizophrenia

You fool,

      you're going to blow your cover.

Why do you

      think you're invincible???

I tell you to

      Run

        R U N   A W A Y

and you go back for more.

Such

A

Pity.

    You could go far

        very far

if you would

      just listen

        to me.

Random thoughts pt. 4

The limitation of my vocabulary

disallows me to elaborate

any further.

< >

I welcome the dark

to ease me out from the day,

bringing me down

from the hot summer sun.

Plenty of faces and places,

old and new,

to amuse me tonight.

Hopefully soon

I will take flight

above the dull roar of the city.

Resolve fades to Darkness

Woke up naked in the valley,

unknowing of how it came to pass.

My body ached;

limbs were numb,

as I lay,

face down in the grass.

There I was, with my mind out of order.

The most painful thing...

an inability to exist.

I felt beaten;

I was bleeding;

my gums hurt.

My head was detached from my body,

still spinning and crying.

I was shaking from the cold,

but strangely felt hot.

I had never felt fear like this before,

which sparked a thought.

I need a change.....

Transformation.

Change my view.....

Interpretation.

I will rise above,

you cannot defeat me.

New me,

old habits will die.

Never again will I go awry.

With your copious demands,

I no longer comply.

But then again,

you, my friend,

are too sexy to resist.

Pull up my sleeve;

press on my wrist;

find the perfect vein,

for your poison to persist.

I no longer condemn.

I just want the world

t

o

m

e

l

t

a

w

a

y

once again.

Resolve fades away.

Monster in Me

I look in the mirror
and see a monster
staring back in my eyes,
penetrating me.

I try to fight it,
but it's too quick to react,
it bites me every time.

I try to scream for someone,
but what's the point
with these sound proof walls?

It haunts me.

Every night,
I toss and turn,
and yearn,
to get one good night sleep.

I need to dream

to escape this reality.

It's my only way out.

The monster has stripped me

of my dreams;

my dignity;

my life.

I just hope someday

he will kill me,

and make me feel it.

I just want to feel...

something.

Dear God

Lord,

why must you play this joke on me?

I'm just a joker who wants to be free.

I refuse to live through these

Slow,

Burning,

Uneventful

moments of my life.

I hate waking up

to this empty, robotic world.

It seems I am always sitting   [alone],

incarcerated in my small, suffocating box.

I cast my shadow upon this ugly world,

awaiting the arrival of my other self.

The playful innocence of age,

is perfectly unattainable.

Nothing is sacred anymore.

The beautiful trees that surrounded us,

are all permanently dead.

This life has lost its saving breath.

Is it true?

Will my life be ending soon?

I hope so.

If it not for the cool laughter

of Satan's apostles,

this would have ended long ago.

But now,

I am ready to go.

just a passing fancy

Do not utter another word
        If you please, I would
        like to go. No. Maybe
        tomorrow. I'll just HANG
        for a few more good times.
        What time can we have,
        that hasn't already had us?
            A lost cause. A dying
        fancy. Perched over a black hole,
        of a world of incomprehensible
        precision. A daily confrontation. A
        desperate reach. A pitiful cry for help.
        Ludicrous. Even a dog knows when
        to give up.
                    HA!
                What a world
                What a world

Random thoughts pt. 5

Stoned and alone...

again.

How long it has been,

since I have seen a friend,

and in their merciful eyes,

I inhabit.

< >

Fair game, so it is.

What a shame,

to be here tonight.

< >

I guess I am here for another day,

that time holds me its captive.

King of Lonely Mountain

How lonely it is at the top.

....

But I can hear the cry ....

.... off in the distance.

How do I g

e

t

d

o

w

n from here?

My euphoria is dying,

and taking me with it.

World of Indifference

Every man and woman
for themselves
in this forsaken land,
deep in a state of grief.

Listen to all the sadistic children.
Do you hear
their cries for help,
as they vilify the "unworthy" crowd?

Do you think they are proud
to be a part
of this sanguinary world?

We recreate the sickness that is taught,
with barely a thought,
and now we stand before you,
with visions of massacre
dancing around in our heads.

Salvi, the sanctimonious madman;

Hitler, the brilliant bigot;

Manson's newfound road to fame.

There are countless numbers,

that bring this existence to shame.

Sick

swarming

madness,

vulgar monstrosities.

Hysterical rage roams free.

We are <prisoners>

of this "free" world,

held captive by fear.

Fear, but not fear alone.

Bittersweet revenge,

blissful blade.

We are all relieved by painless tragedy,

and nestled in a web of uncertainty.

Alone

I've lost my mind

to an uncharted level,

I cannot comprehend.

I just want to drift off

and disappear

into my own realm,

where everything is like a dream.

Where I stand against the wind,

rather than the wind

taking me wherever it blows,

and I have no ~wings~ to fly on my own.

I feel so alone.

Not even at home,

do I feel at home.

My body is young,

but my mind is retired.

I am incapable of love,

I cannot give;

I cannot receive;

a mark on life,

never,

will I leave.

Why do I feel like a wretched soul?

The world feels like a feast,

in honor of my sadness.

Lonely and cold,

my soul plunges.

There is no end,

to this black hole.

Call it a void,

if you will.

I spill my heart to you.....

and you laugh.

Why do you laugh?????

You compound my sorrow,

and with every meaningless word you throw,

my faith in humanity dwindles,

and contempt for you grows.

I truly am........

alone.

Trapper Keeper

I lie to others,

but the worst crime

is I lie to myself,

believing it's who I am.

Trapper in disguise,

a keeper of lies,

like a sacred secret.

I make it up as I go along.

If I do it right,

in my head,

I can never be wrong.

The stories I tell,

weaving truth with deception,

perfectly intertwined,

feeding the monster in my twisted mind.

Wrapped up in my binder of fiction,

living with anxiety,

knowing my contents,

uncovered,

will only cause friction.

Colorful pictures

on the outside.

That is all you will see.

Not the war that rages on

within the pages

inside of me.

God's Green Earth

The night draws near,

and in the dark

my future seems..........unclear.

I sit and think of the things

only my mind can,

to pass the time.

My thoughts grow stranger,

and the one thing

that keeps playing over and over

is death,

pillowed by a bed of flowers.

Since death is the only adventure

no man or woman

can know by experience,

or word of mouth,

it seems to be

an attractive opposition

to the repetitive pain and confusion

offered here,

on God's Green Earth.

Attractive, only until its aggressive force

decides your time is up,

and fear,

welling up

from the very depths of your soul,

seizes your mind

and terrorizes your body.

At this moment,

when you are frozen,

staring into the abyss

of its fiery eyes,

then....

and only then,

will you realize, life is precious

here....

On God's Green Earth.

Random thoughts pt. 6

I look for nothing

but eternity.

I'm feeling something

that I cannot see.

It rips right through me

and society.

Got to escape

from this insanity.

Insanity.....

is what it's going to be.

< >

I watch you at night.

I can hear you dreaming.

We belong together.

I know you feel my presence,

because I exist in your shadow.

I am your reflection.

I am your love.

Ho Hum

Trying to slip out of here,

into the next chapter

of life.

Hoping to never be back

in this strife.

It keeps getting worse

as the days repeat.

Repeat

Repeat

Repeat......

My life today

is the same as it was,

back in the day.

I haven't gotten very far.

Up the street and to the bar.

Long ago,
I took a step into a bear trap,
and decided
I'd never step forward again.

So,
here I am
writing this to you,
hoping you don't perform
the monotonous things I do.

Depression

Snap out of it,
it's all in your head.

It could be worse....
you should be grateful
for what you have.

You take yourself
too seriously.
Cheer up!

You're being selfish,
think of others
for a change.

Pop this pill
and it will all go away.

Thanks for the advice.

This is not my choice.
I have never woken up
and thought,
"life will really suck today."

It's like a switch
embedded in my mind,
flipping
on
and
off
depending on which way
the winds of change
blow
in my thoughts.

If you do not suffer
from this crippling condition,
you don't understand it,
and your ignorance shows.

So don't try to tell me
how this should go.

Going, Going, Gone

My nature and indecision

disallow me to form

the creation of me

I have in my head.

The instant I have

this gleaming authority

to power this mind over matter,

All is forgotten

A moment has passed.

One night stand for the lonely mind

Forever will I hold a place for you,

in my heart.

For what we had,

I will always know that love exists.

It may just be one tawdry night

we got together and lusted like animals,

but I felt you cared about tomorrow,

as I did.

I wanted for you as you wanted for me,

to be happy.

With your embrace, I felt this.

Every word that fell from your lips...

...HOT!

They melted me, as I dribbled toward you.

That night, I felt an eternity of fulfillment.

A worry-less entrapment into your life.

I never felt so content,

and never wanted to be anywhere else.

My love

for you

will live on,

after you're gone.

Random thoughts pt. 7

I never wanted to be what I'm not.

All I want, is a whole lot of lovin'

Feast before my eyes.

<>

The beauty

falls from my eyes,

like a sun setting,

slowly, but surely.

<>

I have seen inside your crystal eyes,

granting me a future

unbeknownst to me.

But how perfect it seems,

you show up out of the blue,

into the gray

patchy field,

that seems to be my life.

Work in Progress

Wondering if I should end it.

Easy *flowing*

into rest.

Eternally free,

sounds the best.

Before I leave this sick world,

I would like to confront

the man who made me.

Tell him the reason for my fate.

Tell him how I became

one of those people,

who I hate.

I try to improve myself.

Lighten the thoughts,

in my **darkened** mind,

but I am worn out.

I'm tired of this constant

work in progress.

mom

I see her sometimes,
through my blotted vision.

But she fades
right back into the shadows,
as quickly as she comes.

Her resurface is a reminder
of what she meant to me.
Something I try so hard to forget.

I wonder what it would be like
not to need her affection anymore.

Losing her seemed so....
unnecessary.

She loved me,
took care of me.

When I fell apart,
she picked up the pieces
of my shattered virginity.

But she left.

She simply flew away,
and blended into the wind.

Since then,
I've been raped
time and time again.

Mom....
where are you?

Tell me,
where I can meet you.

I need you now the most.
I have nowhere else
to turn to.

It hurts.

I am a madman,
I scare myself.

When I am high,
sometimes, I am so far up,
I think I can feel you.

I can see your face
inside the moon,
through the smoke drifting
in the starry sky.

Blurry as it is,
you still look perfect to me.

When I look into the eyes
of another entity I encounter,
it's like
I'm looking right at you.

When I love another,

I am loving you.

I honor you,

Forever.

I love you,

Forever.

Pain, the game of Life

The pain and confusion I feel,

is too unreal.

I feel too much,

yet,

I don't feel enough.

I am not tough.

I can't fight my battles,

head on.

This road _____

is much too long,

and my legs are weary.

Some fun this game is.

No armor to fight,

and no freedom to choose.

I thought I could win,

but I knew I would lose.

Random thoughts pt. 8

The eye in the sky
moving so quickly.

Can I ever be that high?

< >

Crazy canteen of our love.
I can drink all night.
Get drunk off the sweet contents
of our mingled blood.

< >

The world swirls life
all around my head,
yet,
here I sit
in an incredibly dead
state of being.

Losing Myself (schizophrenia pt. 2)

My vulnerable mind

is bound to slip.

Get a grip,

G E   T   A   G   R.I.P!

The torture.

I'm falling   a   p   a   r   t.

Pull-yourself-together!

Persona is an art.

Look in the mirror....

Tell me what you see.

All it is,

before my eyes,

is me

in a clever disguise.

Scenes from a Notebook

73

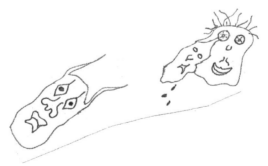

I hate repetition I hate repetion I hate
repetition I hate repetition I
hate repetition I hate repetition I
repetition I hate repetition I hate
I hate repetion I hate repetition
hate repetion I hate repetition I
hate repetition I hate repetition
I hate repetition I hate repetition
I hate repetition I hate repetition
I hate repetition I hate repetition
I hate repetition I hate repetition
I hate repetition I hate repetition
I hate repetition I hate repetition
I hate repetition I hate repetition
I hate repetition I hate repetition
I hate repetition I hate repetition
I hate repetition I hate repetition
I hate repetition I hate repetition
I hate repetition I hate repetition
I hate repetition I hate repetition
I hate repetition I hate repetition
I hate repetition I hate repetition
I hate repetition I hate repetition
I hate repetition I hate repetition
I hate repetition I hate repetition
I hate repetition I hate repetition
I HATE REPE— I hate repeti

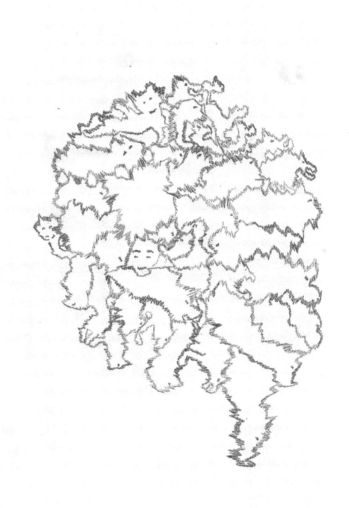

Make up your Mind

Where am I?

Lost.

Can you find me?

Who am I?

Nobody.

Are you with me?

My faith is gone,

no direction.

Who can take care of me?

I am sick of the doubt,

Confusion;

Envy;

The world is against me.

Why?

You've never loved me.

My mind is twisted,

it hurts.

Don't ignore me!

I am going to surrender.

No, you're not.

Keep fighting!

Loving pain

is sickness.

Deceiving gain

is hope.

Give me power?

What a joke!

Everything I desire

I come up short.

I light a cigarette

to **blacken** my **lungs.**

Blacken my SOUL.

Choke me, slowly.

Hang me, kill me.

Take me down

with you.

Let me LIVE

God damn you.

Take the wine,

drown me.

I was dying....

Dying!

Why'd you save me?

Bathe me,

teach me.

Love me,
slave for me.

Beat me,
rid yourself of me.

Carry me,
drop me.
Pick me up,
drop me again.

Save me.

From me.

From my life.

Drunken Conversation in my Head

You lush....

incarnate fool,

get out of my head,

you're spinning out of control.

I told you to have a little fun,

not take my body and run.

Good idea, have another.

It matters not,

that my head is spinning.

This is a party,

keep it rolling,

you are winning!

You're grasping on to something

that felt sacred.....once.

Twice, it wears you down.

Thrice, it gets old,

and anything after

is a nightmare.

Every night with you
is a night to forget,
drenched in a pool
of beer and sweat.
Consuming ale after ale,
shots and stouts.
While inordinate people
buzz about.

Each drink
you hammer down
is changing me.
My thoughts are no longer
in my control,
or even slightly
intelligible.

I know you think
you're a sly creation,
but what you are
is an embarrassment
of the entire nation.

Nature of Despair

Racing through life with child's eyes,

while ministers disencumber our fears,

with soft spoken lies.

Father's orgasm is over,

our children are damaged goods.

What good is a world

with an all-powerful God,

when the unwelcomed guest

still lingers.

Pay attention,

because death is merging on our left.

Death speaks LOUDLY, with life under its breath.

Creeping closer toward us,

perfecting its plan.

Once it hits the mark,

you realize,

we are all just man.

No do-overs,

no turning back.

When it decides

your time is up...

no matter how hard the fight,

you're already gone.

I just hope your journey

was long.....

enough.

Head Gum

Things constantly get stuck
in my unsuspecting mind.
Although they're never invited,
upon arrival,
I fail to decline.

In the moment,
I don't really care,
as it serves as a distraction
from the life I can't bear.

They enter my thoughts
and procreate.
Quickly they fester,
then saturate.

I try to rise above
and transcend the clatter,
but it wins the battle
for control of grey matter.

The gum in my head,
I keep chewing away.
It mucks up the motor
and leads me astray.

When I'm about to breakthrough,
on an important matter,
something insignificant
finds room in my head.

It rattles around
like a pinball machine
til the initial thought
is completely dead.

It's all just a bunch of noise,
but my lack of poise
keeps me reeling
and strips my body
of emotional feeling.

The
Endless.Mindless
NoIsE,
keeps playing with my head,
like a giant child
playing with his toys.

I've stopped trying to fight,
it never goes away,
but I do wonder sometimes,
who keeps hitting play?

It's like a never-ending infomercial
advertising hell.

I imagine down south,
peace of mind
never sees the light of day,
and this is not a place
that I care to stay.

Land of the ___
Lost

People strive to be a mystery,

which makes it easier

to figure them out.

The amazing thing is,

people can become

what they long to be.

But achieving this

brings shameful regret,

stuck in a self-imposed trap.

Ironic!

Once Formed, Never Returned.

This is your brain on drugs....

any questions?

My brain is an egg,
cracked and fried,
and the ensuing damage
hardly seems worth
this carnival ride.

Defeated by the fact
that there is no cure.
Just a daily struggle,
resisting allure.

Fragile like the egg
with a delicate shell.
~~~~~~~~~~~~~~~~~~~~~~~~~~~
Destruction of mind,
results in total loss of will.

Turns out,

the devil needed my help

to fund this bill...

and I obliged.

Confusion;

Anger;

Resentment;

Shame;

This is your brain on drugs.

Without question.

Random thoughts pt. 9

Anger built up

to make a wall

under which

you will fall.

< >

Truly true

I say to you,

it's a mess up here

in the attic.

< >

If I died tomorrow,

would you cry for me today?

Note to Self

I let life get the best of me.
The best of my days,
which turn to years.

The whispers in my head,
are like silent tears.

You should quiet the noise,
you foolish man.
Your days are numbered,
you're a flash in the pan.

Your petty grievances,
will drive you insane.
You'll crash and burn,
like a spiraling plane.

You've fed those demons,
long enough.

Starve them now,

you've had enough.

The pain cuts like a dull knife,

through your flesh,

slowly,

sinking deeper.

Sliding through your tissue,

ripping your muscle.

Inch

by

Inch.

Soon,

there will be nothing left.

The Breeze

Countryside.

Beautiful legs,

open wide.

In you,

I confide.

I'm a product

of your seduction.

You're the object

of my destruction.

But you continue to tease,

and I ask you please,

keep it hot.....

don't let in

the breeze.

Hypnotized

Pleasure just beyond my eyes,

I cannot reach,

I'm hypnotized.

Throughout my body,

there lies a truth.

But I cannot handle

that reality.

I've never known

what it's like

to be loose.

I shrink

at the sound of laughter.

I walk through life

without purpose.

The lord,
I seek destroyed.

My life,
I seek employed.

I cannot wake up,
no matter how hard I try,
I'm hypnotized.

Out of Sight

I can see

through the blind man,

that our future is darkness.

We must walk through these halls,

with our hands out.

All that I am,

and want to be,

is a shot in the dark...

a gamble.

I long to have ability to see,

or for someone

to take care of me.

A service dog

to lead me through life.

Without this,

I keep walking into walls,

and I've never found a door

to the outside world.

Corrugated Mess

My life in boxes,
packed away.

The mess inside.

Where do I begin to find
the things
I've tried to hide.

Unpacking the puzzle,
from a lifetime of being a dog
quieted by a muzzle.

Squares and rectangles,
tangle,
tangled up inside.

Constantly moving to avoid settling in,
afraid to confide.

The boxes I bring with me

everywhere I go.

The contents remain intact,

but never to show.

Although I know that show and tell,

is where I would begin to see,

the full picture

of the puzzling boxes,

when put together,

is me.

Random thoughts pt. 10

Like a desert, void of life,

are my surroundings.

But somewhere in the distance,

a whisper,

so loud in my head,

is hounding me to just take

a few more steps.

< >

I will,

for the sake of me,

forgive myself,

and I'll be free.

Time Consumption

Life presumes,

and consumes me.

Each breath takes away

another second

I had to live,

and to prosper....

to make something happen.

When all this time,

It's right there happening.

Fate

Life is just an act to follow,
and this is not a rehearsal.

Beautify your surroundings,
they tell you.
Make yourself fit to be king.

What a shameful lie!

We all hold the truth
within ourselves,
but we keep it concealed,
away from the world.

The drama of it all
(((((((((holds us)))))))))
in the deep-rooted
confusion we are in.

Entertainment
is driving this bus.

We all need the drama,
to subside our feelings of guilt
and self-loathing.

Another's pain
is a ticket to the show.

I need to shed
these fateful actions,
and form my own being.

But I continue
to follow suit.

It seems,
I'll never truly be satisfied
with that sense of loss,
for a better gain.

Bloodbath (pieces of me)

Life is shattering,
and until the sky opens up
and swallows me whole,
I will remain little fragments of me.

I've changed my personality
so many times now,
I can't even remember
who I am anymore.

Trying to hold my pieces together
is like trying to win a war.

Me against the world.

What a bloodbath
this has been.

Just a thought

The days pass on,
and all is well.....

.....kept inside me.

The better it gets,
the more difficult
it seems to become.

But I strive toward
a deeper meaning of life.

I work for self-gain,
is that selfish?

All the knowledge in the world
will not help my soul.

But will it hurt it?

Material happiness
is not the key to a world
of love and peace
within my mind.

Simplicity makes the heart flourish.

Greed disengaged our potential unification,
yet this terror seems to be
a pleasurable experience,
for most.

So,
I wait and wonder
and contemplate my motives.

The days keep passing on.

Random thoughts pt. 11

I've always had a good train of thought,

but can't completely work out the kinks.

I guess I was never

well taught,

to properly think.

< >

My head is splitting,

I'm falling in.

I can't get out,

and I cannot swim.

< >

I travel through this world,

like I travel through my mind.

In both,

I am lost.

Impossible to find.

Peaceful Light

Your peaceful light turns to night.

You feel just right in that state of mind.

Running from your crystal fear,

over there,

behind your wall,

where the demons call,

and angels fight for an awakening of your soul.

I wonder if you can see

the subtlety

in which you feed the lions,

to keep on flying,

over falls,

beyond those walls,

just for another day in which you pay

to stay high upon this pillowed sky.

Blind to the fact

that you,

really are,

you.

Precious Freight

What do you do

when love slips away,

and what do you say

when God asks you to pray?

My mind is deteriorating,

thoughts don't seem real anymore.

My feelings get trampled

and I feel like a whore,

giving myself to anybody

who sees an opportunity

to walk

through my unlocked door.

Take my heart and run.

It does not matter

that you were my only sun.

I'll sit here in the dark.

Pay no attention

to my tears.

All they are is a window

to my life,

my love...

my fears.

I will refrain from expressing myself.

I would never ask you to listen

to my words.

They only speak wisdom from life,

I have learned.

For love,

I will remain in wait.

But until then,

I will continue to be the rail

underneath your train,

carrying my endless cargo of emotion,

and precious freight.

Dear God pt. 2

What will it take

with

me

and

you?

I am feeling lost

in my unstable mind.

I don't know if I can hold on

to whatever sanity I have left.

With each passing day

the confusion grows,

befouling my head.

I have a feeling the "being"

inside of me

will someday takeover

and no longer let me see myself,

as I truly am....

I watch myself do these crazy things
and have no control.

Am I that disconnected
from the innocence
I once adored?

What would it take
to repossess that simple,
yet,
invaluable pleasure
of a child living pure and honestly
in the world?

Please God,
do not let me waste away like this.
Let me shine.

My light is bright enough
to show the way down any path,
but I have been dimming
for too long now.

Let me out of this contract
I seem to have signed
somewhere down the line.

Show me the way
to a brighter day.

Commander in Chief

Commander sir,
look down on your faithful warriors.
Have pity on their last peaceful lay on earth.

In a few short hours,
they will help you quench
this bloodthirsty world.

Choose carefully, Commander sir,
the weight of a thousand men
has been thrust upon your shoulders.

The pressure is building,
you're deranged with that pathetic smile.

But do not give in
to your weary character.

Let the night entertain your fears.

Mother nature will control you
with her clever illusions.

All eyes are on your brilliant plan.
You simply cannot let these people down.

How can your guilty vision look
upon those victimized, ardent people.
Your men are blinded with reason,
eagerly awaiting their Armageddon.

Do you remember love...
...and comfort?
Playing with your brothers,
the grace of your mother?

Such simple things enthralled you,
and kept you warm within your paradise.
But that part of your life is over.

Go quietly now,
the sun is rising.
Succumb to your hard-earned tragedy.

A thought to process

Sliding

swerving

panic.

Like a monster

devouring the calm

that a second before,

kept me at peace.

The feeling of imminent death,

gasping at what was possibly,

my last breath.

The relentless rain

took control of the tires

which once held occupation

on the road beneath me.

As I went flailing into the dark,

in a state of acceptance,

I closed my eyes.

An enormous jolt
and the simultaneous sound
of metal on metal
sent a chill down my spine.

I sat there in the dark,
motionless.

I waited to be lifted,
floating freely
through the infinite skies.

But nothing happened.

I looked out and saw a hundred eyes
fixated on my misfortune,
curiously wondering if my life
had expired.

While things settled,
I did some wondering of my own.

I wondered why some

are more fortunate than others.

What makes me special,

or gives me the right to stay here

for another day

over another?

Like, for instance...

my mother.

Everything in life

must have a purpose.

Every life has meaning......

What is mine?

Monopoly Money

People monopolizing people.

Erecting their capital,
building their lavish malls.
Living in their oversized abodes,
with empty corridors.

Shielded by their lies,
shrouded in the notion
of their pristine steeple,
and its powerful potion.

The province,
they deny,
a taste of milk and honey.

Hoarding their fortune,
like humanity is a game.

Monopoly money.

For the impoverished;

the sick;

this illusion of grandeur

is an intimidating trick.

They must never pass go,

and the powerful grow.

It belittles the mind,

and when you're mentally weak,

you abuse your body,

which crushes your soul.

And underneath that rock

is the perpetual goal.

Journey to Nowhere

One day walking along,
I fell and bumped my head
on a giant rock.

After I laid there,
in and out of consciousness,
for what seemed an eternity,
the wind gently whispered by my ear,
alleviating me from the dry hot air.

It spoke to me,
softly,
giving me motivation to get on my feet.
Hope.

Then, out of nowhere,
a beautiful stream, glistening from the sun,
just appeared.

My chance for revival.

My glands started to salivate

for the first time in hours.

Natures sweet nectar...

Water...

Life!

When I arrived,

the stream faded to nothing,

leaving me with but a mouthful of sand...

...and shattered hopes.

Much.Like.Life.

Don't

You

Think?

Gentle rain, wash away my tears

Have you ever been outside and crying,

and the rain was gently

p   u   i   g

o   r   n

d   w

o   n

from the heavens,

washing away the wounds

from a callous land?

The rain,

cleansing your eyes,

and clearing the way

to see,

through the clarity of wisdom,

a world of impossibility.

The moment I see the sun peeking out

from beyond the clouds,

I see the meaning of life,

without a doubt.

To find the light

in the darkness,

and to know

even though

I am cold and wet,

the warmth will be there,

soon enough.

I've only seen a glimpse

of that eternal light

that will someday,

hopefully,

set me free.

I ask you,

God,

when will that sunlight,

shine down on me?

Internal Soldier

You act tough,

but have a secret fear,

of an uncertainty.

Fear that is crippling,

and feels impossible

to come to terms with.

Come forth from the armor

you've been living in.

Do not hide your wounds

anymore.

Show them precisely as they are.

Be vulnerable.

Tell your internal soldier

to keep trudging

through your swampy ideas.

The fear may paralyze you at times,

but will make you courageous

in the end.

You reside

in your comfortable darkness,

but let the light shine on you,

for once,

like you deserve.

Show the world

that beautiful smile.

The Big Screen

I guard my inner-self,

for my use only.

Not to be released

on the big screen.

I allow little previews,

here and there.

But my story sticks

to the core of my own soul,

and tears it apart.

Leaving me a giant piece

of

ab

str

act

art.

mercy, mercy me

Is it true what they say,
will life really be ok?

Will everything just,
"fall into place"?

Am I going to stay afloat,
in this watered-down rat race?

Will I find love.....
a love supreme, from up above,
to carry me and make sure I stay on track?

Can I make it alone,
if I had to?

Will I ever recover,
or will I suffer my bad choices?

Is success evident upon
things you can touch and see,
or does it really exist somewhere inside me?

If it is locked somewhere inside my heart,
who the hell has the key,
that will someday set me free
from these chains that burden my soul?

I have no answers,
but I do know one thing.....

The world is beautiful,
along with its people, places
and things.

But, nothing like the infinite
realm of the heavens.

God, have mercy on our souls

Intimate Garden

Thin clouds of smoke circulate my head,

and a nauseating feeling

settles in my stomach.

It chews away at my soul

a little more each day.

Time continues to slide by my tired,

anxious eyes.

I wonder when it will happen.

When my hands will start to work

in my favor.

When I will lift above this cloud

and look down on my kingdom

and smile with ease.

Admire the seeds

in which I have planted,

for you and me.

The seeds of life,

that grow an intimate garden.

The garden,

that should grow in all of us.

Old Friend

I took another look

upon

his face,

br oke n once again.

His pupils were small,

and eyes

were dull and lifeless.

He looked at me,

possibly pondering a time

when we had shared

the misery behind

the mask he wears.

His old accomplice,

now lying in a pine box

he had built for himself,

streams through his mind.

Loneliness surges through his heart,

like an intense wave.

He looks to me

with a plan,

an indirect approach,

a cry for someone

to help him hide.

A need for someone there,

unbearable need,

for someone to use,

to abuse.

Support system,

for drug addiction.

I played with the idea,

for a good

twenty minutes.

I thought of

what I stand to lose,

or what I could possibly gain.

I thought of the scars
I've left behind.

The tears,
the shame,
the lying I did
to get high, as I

S
I
i
d down deeper
into the grips
of a dark world.

As I drove away
that night,
I breathed a sigh of relief,
and awoke this morning
feeling good about life.

140

Jaw$

We are not a lost cause.

We are not trapped

between the massive jaws,

pulling

us

down

through the depths

of despair.

It feels that way,

but we just need to remember

p for air.

to come u

We all have a chance

to fight our way through.

Swim through the tides

and find the beacon of light,

guiding us to the promised land.

Sanctuary

A silly poem dedicated to my old friend, Wendy K.

An Indian dance in the early morning grog,

tango with the curtains.

A banana rots,

while stomachs cave in from their neglect.

Preacher in his glory,

long and furious ride.

Olives and cream,

tonight, we miss out on our dreams.

Lemon and honey taste so good,

but it could never happen.

Uncontrollable fits of laughter,

reality has no meaning anymore.

Candles burning for my soul,

taxi man, come relieve my burden.

Disappointment and quiet time,

please don't leave me with my mind.

Almost made it to my sanctuary,

I'll get there soon....

I guess.

Just the two of us

Perhaps a little later

    w

  e   e

   w   s

    i   i

    l   r

    l   a

And try to find ourselves

    Without confrontation

        Or............Delay.

But for now, it's just another day,

    To be free

      Of worry

And oddly shaped creatures

    Of the universe.

      Just

      The

      Two

      Of

      Us.

Just
The Two
of US

Perhaps a little later
We will arise
and Try to find ourselves,
without Confrontations
or delay.
BuT for now, it's another day
To be free
                of worry,
and oddly shaped creatures
        of The universe.
JusT The Two of US.

144

Ryanne

Laughter, song and dance,
and a touch of sweet romance,
from your fingers to my heart,
make every day worth a start.

Bringing a smile to your face,
or easing your pain with a warm embrace;
to live and love,
and go out to play,
with you,
brings meaning to my life.

Life is too short,
time devours the minutes
that make up the day.

But you, my inamorata,
so lovely...
I love to lay by your side,
into the languid night,
pulling the wool o'er our eyes.

Miles between us

We have many towns,

trees,

miles of brush,

rivers,

even an ocean,

between us right now.

Which seems

as far

as the moon.

But your face,

ever so etched in my mind,

is beautiful.

I can close my eyes,

and picture you perfectly.

Which makes the moon

not seem

so far.

Poison Fruit

"Let it be"

to me,

he spoke.

The tree bears fruit

containing desire,

not fulfillment.

Come and eat the fruit

unto which I bear,

and you

shall be fulfilled.

The little boy in the sand

My child,

I come to you

to beg

for your forgiveness.

I have come to the river of peace,

to find you standing there,

so innocent,

looking up at me,

with those wonderous eyes.

I marvel at your strength.

Such a small child,

with that beautiful smile.

Come laugh with me,

and walk a mile down this beach,

toward the sunset.

Talk to me,

tell me about you.

Tell me how you can smile,

so confident about life.

How were we parted from each other,

so long ago?

I love you so much.

The sun will bring us warmth,

and comfort.

Come splash the water with me,

and we will be one,

once again.

Final Thought

There's an evil
that's calling us
to climb aboard.

It's a long road home.

It's up to us
if we ride that bus.....

or walk the distance.

Acknowledgments

There have been so many influential people in my life through the years, too many to mention. If you have touched my life, you know who you are and how, just know that I love you all.

Mike, Kim, Sarah & Chrissy, you are my second family. You have always been good to me. When I went through one of the worst times in my life, you stuck by me without flinching. You're all amazing, I love you guys!

Mom, I know you have been there with me all along, so you have seen my thoughts and you know how I feel about you. I will see you again someday. Until then, you will continue to be in my thoughts and prayers. Love you to heaven and back.

Dad, if it were not for you, I would not be here today, and I firmly believe that. Your sobriety was certainly challenged, especially in the early stages, but you did it. You stuck to it, and as a result, helped me find mine. No matter how many times I fell, you were there. I love you, Mr. Sidekick.

Mary, Cathy & Julie, we have been apart for so long now, it is hard to even recall the days we were together, happily playing with whatever fad was sweeping the nation, or silly games we played outside, or annoying our neighbor with the 64 cats! But those are some of the fondest memories I have in life. Whenever we reunite, I am on cloud nine. I love you all to no end.

Immaculate Conception School, even though you are a thing of the past (mine and in general), I feel like I need to mention you here. Best school ever!

To my children, Emmalina, Peyton, Finnian & Charlotte, you are my pride and joy. You all showed me how to love again, as with you, it came so naturally. I love each of you for different reasons, the little personalities you all have are adorable. I love you all, with all of my heart

Rye, the love of my life, what can I even say? There are no words. You are the most amazing person I have ever met. 20+ years of being married to me, I believe qualifies you for sainthood. I love you to the moon and back, no matter what.

Last, but certainly not least, I want to thank God. My true father and savior.

About the Author

Thomas was born and raised in suburban Massachusetts with his father, stay at home mother, and three sisters. He was raised Catholic, attending a private Catholic School in his early childhood years.

When he was 11 years old, his parents separated for the last time, opting to divorce after 16+ years of a very stormy marriage. His father, an admitted alcoholic, having relapsed and still active at that time, was left at the childhood home which was in foreclosure. Thomas moved to a new town with his mother and three sisters. He then started to attend a local public school in the 6th grade, where he felt lost and disconnected from the rest of the kids. Public schooling is vastly different from private Catholic schooling, which resulted in a couple of extremely lonely years. Having no friends during this time, his mother was the lighthouse in an ocean of pain left by the separation, divorce, and relocation.

When he was 13 years old, his mother died instantly in a car crash on her way to her graduate program where she was completing her studies to become a nurse. Her sudden death resulted in his estranged father reentering his life as sole caretaker. At this point, his father had stopped drinking once again but was only a few months sober, and trying to get his life in order.

Being in a place of pain and confusion, Thomas turned to drugs and alcohol at the age of 14.

Going to St John's High School (a renowned school) was his mother's dream for him and just five months after her sudden death, he began attending. After completing just one year, he left that school, making a choice to be closer to his friends to boost his social life, and attended a vocational high school in Marlborough, MA that was well known for overwhelming drug use and partying. Pain, confusion, and disarray in his life escalated substantially.

When he was 15, he accidentally overdosed on an excessive amount of alcohol, as a result of using cocaine which he was introduced to at a party. When paramedics arrived, his heart had stopped and one lung had collapsed, leaving him on the brink of death. After which, he had slipped into a comatose state for 2+ days. Upon recovery and returning home from the hospital, he was mandated to appear before a judge due to this incident. The judge then ordered that he attend a drug/alcohol rehabilitation program, which he completed and returned home.

A year later, after tearing up the neighborhood and causing considerable damage to property in a display of displaced anger with a few friends, he once again appeared before a judge who was considering remanding him over to the state, removing him from his father's custody. In a plea to maintain custody, his father then agreed to get him help and placed in a program for troubled teens in Lawrence, MA where he stayed for several months, which is where he found poetry through various fellow teenagers in that drug abuse facility. There was one very special counselor there that was able to "break through" the huge wall of armor that he had formed about himself. He started to write voraciously from that point on. Stuck in his own head and feeling that he can't relate to the world around him in a true sense, he never went anywhere without a pen and notebook.

Throughout much of his teen years, he was in and out of various treatment facilities and halfway houses for behavioral issues, much of which involved drug and alcohol abuse. Due to a strained relationship with his father, he became homeless on a couple of occasions as a runaway. One stint ended up across the country in San Francisco where he was sucked into a methamphetamine world.

When he was 21, an arrest involving driving a stolen car with a suspended license along with drugs found on his person, lead to several months in jail. This proved to be an "opportunity" to learn some very important lessons through yet another special counselor that he encountered through a program that he opted to go through while incarcerated.

His writings reveal the enormous struggle with the immense "dark" times that he experienced through his tumultuous teen years.

Thomas is now living in Oregon with his wife of over 20 years and 4 children.

Printed in the USA
CPSIA information can be obtained
at www.ICGtesting.com
LVHW091352280224
773024LV00056B/1350